The New Laws of Power

The Code for Winning in a World that Keeps Changing

by

BRIAN TURNER

This book is a work of nonfiction. While it references historical events, policies, and systemic patterns, any personal anecdotes or illustrative narratives are used for explanatory purposes. The views expressed are those of the author and are intended for informational and educational discussion. The book does not constitute legal, financial, or investment advice.

For permissions requests, inquiries, or more information, contact:

Published by HEY BBT LLC
https://heybbt.com

ISBN (Paperback): *978-1-971050-18-8*
ISBN (Hardcover): *978-1-971050-19-5*
ISBN (eBook): *978-1-971050-17-1*

First Edition

Printed in the United States

Table of Contents

Epigraph

"A people without the knowledge of their past history, origin, and culture is like a tree without roots."
Marcus Garvey

Prologue: Why This Book Exists

Power has never changed, only the arenas. Rome rose on discipline and collapsed on excess. The same pattern echoes in hip hop: artists build empires from nothing, then watch them collapse under ego, greed, or betrayal. The arenas change, battlefields, boardrooms, or music, but the laws remain the same. Those who refuse to learn them are erased by them.

The rules of the past no longer apply.
Homes once sold for pennies on the dollar. Steady careers lasted decades. Loyalty was rewarded with pensions and security that could endure for generations. The path was not always easy, but at least it existed.

That world is gone.

The ground now shifts without warning.

- The dot-com boom created overnight millionaires and erased them.
- September 11th revealed how a single morning could reshape the global order.
- The 2008 financial collapse swallowed homes, jobs, and generational wealth.
- Social media turned attention into currency and the fastest way to self-destruction.
- A global pandemic locked entire societies down and rewrote economies.

Centuries ago, empires rose and fell over generations. Today, entire industries collapse in a matter of years. Banks that once seemed untouchable vanish in months. Businesses that dominate a decade often disappear before the next decade. Stability has been replaced with volatility, and predictability has become a myth.

Playing by the rules, doing everything "right," no longer guarantees survival.

Case Study: The Collapse of Certainty

For decades, Fannie Mae was treated like a vault. It carried the weight of government backing and the reputation of permanence. Savings flowed into it. Retirements depended on it. Families believed it was the one investment that could not fail.

Then came the rise of mortgage-backed securities. Home loans, once stable, boring assets, were packaged, sold, and leveraged until the system became a tower built on sand. When the housing bubble burst, the illusion of safety vanished. Fannie Mae crumbled under the very securities it was built to support.

What had seemed unshakable dissolved into chaos. Accounts emptied. Confidence collapsed. The symbol of stability became proof of fragility.

The lesson: no pillar is permanent. What feels untouchable today can be rubble tomorrow.

Case Study: The Mirage of Online Trading

At the same time, online trading emerged as the new gold rush. Conferences filled with eager investors who believed the future was finally in their hands. The atmosphere was electric, with charts projected on giant screens and speakers promising a new era of democratized wealth. Anyone with a computer and courage could supposedly win.

For a while, it worked. Accounts doubled. Success stories spread like wildfire. People mortgaged homes and emptied savings to go all in.

Then the bubble burst. Overnight, those glowing screens turned red. Fortunes evaporated in hours. The same traders who had bragged of independence now faced ruin.

The lesson is as old as ambition itself: **hype is the most dangerous trap in power; it makes people sprint faster toward the cliff without noticing the edge. Speed without structure is how power destroys itself.**

The classic works on power explain how emperors, generals, and rulers survived in their eras. But today's battlefield looks different. Distraction has become a new form of slavery. Algorithms can silence voices. Entire industries vanish between paychecks.

In this world, intelligence is not enough. Hard work is not enough. Hope is not enough.

What is required is a different kind of armor: the discipline to expect nothing, the restraint to master emotion, the patience to move quietly, the discernment to choose battles, and the foresight to think beyond the moment. These are survival mechanics, not slogans.

This is not self-help. This is survival.
This is not motivation. This is mechanics.

What follows is a manual, a code, a set of laws forged for instability, written for a generation that inherited volatility yet must still find a way to win.

These are the New Laws of Power: the code for winning in a world that keeps changing.

Part 0: Shifts That Broke the Old Rules

"He who has conquered himself is a far greater hero than he who has defeated a thousand times a thousand men."
Buddha

Chapter 1: Ancient Power

Empires were never sustained by ideals alone. Ideals inspire. Discipline governs. They rose through discipline, restraint, and control, and they collapsed when those qualities eroded. Rome built its strength on the order of its legions, only to rot from within when indulgence replaced sacrifice.

Hip hop proved the same truth. Ownership, not talent, determined who endured. The ones who signed away control, no matter how talented, often became cautionary tales.

Sun Tzu taught that wars were decided before the first strike, by patience, deception, and structure. The Stoics, from Epictetus to Marcus Aurelius, warned that no throne was secure if the ruler could not master himself.

From the battlefield to the palace to the studio, the law repeats: **power begins with control, and it ends the moment control is lost.**

The Roots of Strategy

Rome expanded because its armies were organized and its citizens disciplined. But decadence hollowed it from within.
Sparta thrived by raising warriors through restraint, not comfort.
In China, Sun Tzu revealed that control of perception could defeat armies without ever drawing a sword.
Stoics like Marcus Aurelius and Epictetus taught that the first empire to conquer is the self.

Every tradition arrived at the same conclusion: control precedes power.

Case Study: Rome's Decay

In its early centuries, Rome's discipline was unmatched. Soldiers built roads as efficiently as they conquered territories. Citizens were expected to serve, sacrifice, and endure hardship. Power grew because restraint was enforced at every level of society.

But as wealth poured in, discipline eroded. The elite feasted while the legions weakened. Bread and circuses distracted the masses while corruption rotted the Senate. Rome no longer controlled itself, and so it could no longer control its empire.

Rome did not fall because it was conquered from the outside. It fell because it surrendered control from within.

The Oldest Form of Power: Slavery

No empire flourished without it. Rome built monuments, roads, and wealth on the backs of slaves. Egypt's pyramids were raised through generations of forced labor. To rulers, slavery was not merely economics; it was proof of dominance, the ability to own time, bodies, and futures.

Centuries later, American slavery continued the same principle. This system extended beyond the whip and the chain. It was psychological, cultural, and generational. Language was stolen. Families were broken. Dependency was enforced by law. **It was designed not just to control the present, but to sabotage the future**.

Echoes of Slavery

Control systems evolve when force becomes inefficient.

- Debt locks generations into repayment cycles that outlive paychecks.
- Distraction consumes attention, the most valuable resource of all.
- Dependency on jobs, technology, or social approval keeps people obedient without force.

Case Study: The Student Debt Trap

In the modern age, student loans were sold as a ticket to freedom. Education was marketed as the guaranteed path to security. But like Rome's slaves, millions found themselves bound by invisible chains: debt that cannot be escaped, interest that compounds over decades, futures mortgaged before they even began.

What promised liberation became bondage. What was framed as an opportunity became an obligation.

Lesson

From empires to economies, the law has never changed. Control builds empires, and the absence of control destroys them. Those who enforce discipline over armies, societies, or individuals command power. Those who lose it collapse.

The oldest truth remains the clearest: **whoever controls your options controls your future.**

Chapter 2: Modern Earthquakes

History once moved in centuries. Dynasties rose, ruled for generations, and fell slowly under the weight of their own excess. Rome took hundreds of years to collapse. Empires in Asia, Africa, and Europe lasted lifetimes before they crumbled.

Today, collapse happens in real time. Industries vanish in years, movements burn out in months, and reputations evaporate in hours. What once took centuries now happens in shocks.

The same acceleration is visible in culture. Hip hop moguls built empires that seemed untouchable, but in a world moving at the speed of the internet, relevance fades faster than contracts expire. What once took decades to unravel now dissolves in a season.

Those who move slowly are crushed faster.

Case Study: The Dot-Com Boom

In the late 1990s, the internet was hailed as the new frontier. Startups with no profits raised millions. Investors threw money at any company with ".com" in its name. Hype alone became a business model.

One symbol stood out: **pets.com.** The company burned through more than $300 million in under two years, collapsing so fast that its infamous sock-puppet mascot became a symbol of the entire bubble.

When the dot-com bubble burst in 2000, trillions in market value disappeared. Companies once valued higher than established corporations collapsed overnight. Fortunes were erased, workers displaced, and faith in the “new economy” shaken.

Lesson: speed amplifies weakness as quickly as it amplifies success.

Case Study: September 11th

On the morning of September 11, 2001, the illusion of safety evaporated in a cloud of smoke and steel. Planes became weapons, towers crumbled, and the world watched in disbelief.

The aftermath reshaped power far beyond New York. Airports were never the same again. Security that once felt invisible became invasive. Fear restructures power faster than force.

One morning changed geopolitics for decades.

Lesson: power is fragile when security is assumed.

Case Study: The 2008 Collapse

Homes were once the foundation of American stability. Families bought into the promise of ownership and security. But beneath it lay the unstable structure of mortgage-backed securities. Loans were packaged, sold, and resold until no one understood the risk.

The collapse of **Lehman Brothers**, a 158-year-old firm, became the symbol of fragility. If a bank that old could fail overnight, nothing was safe.

When the housing bubble burst, the collapse rippled through banks, markets, and entire nations. People who "did everything right" lost houses, jobs, and futures.

Lesson: following the rules offers no protection when the rules themselves are corrupt.

Case Study: The Social Media Trap

In 2007, the iPhone put the internet in every pocket. Platforms like Facebook, Instagram, and Twitter turned attention into the most valuable currency. Anyone could broadcast to the world. Anyone could be famous.

But visibility without vision became a trap. Platforms rose and fell with breathtaking speed. **MySpace, once the king of social media, vanished**

almost overnight. Vine, once the future of video, disappeared in six years.

The race for likes, followers, and clout created dependence. Attention became addictive, fleeting, and fragile. Those who built lives on algorithms became owned by them..

Lesson: attention is power, but dependence on attention is slavery.

Case Study: The Pandemic Reset

In 2020, a virus did what wars and governments could not: it shut the world down. Borders closed, economies stalled, and lives were redefined. Jobs disappeared overnight. Industries adapted or died.

New empires emerged in weeks. **Zoom became the new town square, growing from 10 million daily users to over 300 million in less than a year.** Companies that had been afterthoughts became essential. Those who waited for the world to "return to normal" discovered there was no normal to return to.

Lesson: power belongs to the adaptable, not the comfortable.

Lesson

Modern earthquakes prove one truth: volatility is the environment. Power now belongs to those who adapt before collapse announces itself. Each collapse: dot-com hype, terror, financial ruin, social addiction, or pandemic, revealed the same truth: stability is an illusion.

Volatility is not the exception. It is the environment.

Chapter 3: The Future Storm

Empires have always collapsed when the future arrived faster than they could prepare for it. Rome fed itself on the grain of conquered lands, but when supply lines broke and harvests failed, famine weakened the empire before the barbarians ever breached its gates. The Black Death erased a third of Europe's population, ending feudal systems that had stood for centuries. In the 20th century, oil shocks revealed that nations were not powered by ideals, but by the scarcity of fuel.

History once moved in centuries. Now it moves in shocks. The future will not arrive gently, but violently, in overlapping waves of change. Each storm will erase the illusion of stability faster than the last. The future punishes preparation delay more than ignorance.

The same acceleration is visible in culture. Hip hop showed how quickly empires could rise and vanish. Record labels, fashion lines, and media platforms that seemed permanent in one decade became irrelevant in the next. Physical albums became digital files, then streams, then playlists controlled by algorithms. And now AI is beginning to compose beats, mimic voices, and generate songs at scale. The culture that once crowned artists now experiments with replacing them.

What took Rome centuries now happens in seasons. The future will not be defined by one disruption, but by storms that collide all at once.

Case Study: The AI Revolution

Machines once replaced hands. Now they replace minds. Artificial intelligence is rewriting the definition of work, value, and creativity. Entire industries, from law to design to medicine, are being rebuilt in real time.

The storm is not the technology itself, but the speed. Those who adapt will multiply their leverage. Resisting will not preserve dignity; it will accelerate irrelevance.

Lesson: in the age of AI, learning fast is more valuable than knowing much.

Case Study: Crypto and Decentralization

For centuries, banks controlled trust. Crypto promised to break that monopoly. Millions bought in, convinced they were part of a revolution. Fortunes were made, and fortunes were lost.

The volatility exposed the truth: decentralization removes intermediaries, not responsibility, Power is shifting from central institutions to distributed networks.

Lesson: the future will not be controlled by a single system, but by whoever understands the systems best.

Case Study: Climate and Resources

Empires have always risen and fallen with resources. Water, land, oil: these were the foundations of power. The coming century will be no different. Droughts, floods, and shortages will redraw borders, ignite wars, and decide which nations thrive or collapse.

The greatest resource will not be land or oil, but adaptability to scarcity.

Lesson: the strongest survive not by abundance, but by preparing for scarcity.

Case Study: Attention Saturation

The future economy will not be built only on money, but on attention. Yet attention is already stretched thin. Every scroll, every notification, every video competes for the same seconds of human focus.

Platforms rise fast and die faster. Today's empire can vanish in a trend cycle. In a storm of infinite noise, silence and clarity will become rare, and therefore powerful.

Lesson: attention is the currency, but clarity is the leverage.

Lesson

The future will not be a single event. It will be an overlapping storm of technology, decentralization, scarcity, and saturation. The future will arrive unevenly and without warning. Those who prepare for single disruptions will fail. Those who build for constant instability will endure.

Power in the future belongs to the adaptable, the disciplined, and the early.

Part I – The Inner Game

"Blessed is he who expects nothing, for he shall never be disappointed."
Alexander Pope

LAW 1: The Zero Expectation

Power is lost the moment you believe the world owes you *anything*.

History

Julius Caesar believed Brutus would never turn on him. Brutus was not just an ally but a protégé, almost a son. When whispers of betrayal reached him, Caesar dismissed them; he expected loyalty.

On the Ides of March, daggers found his flesh in the Senate. The final wound, history tells us, came when Brutus struck. Caesar's last words were not rage but disbelief: "Et tu, Brute?" Expectation blinded him until his dying breath.

From Caesar's fall to Alexander the Great's fractured empire to Chinese dynasties undone by heirs, history repeats the same lesson: power anchored to expectation collapses.

The same truth was revealed in slavery. Enslaved people who expected mercy from masters, or fairness from the system, lived in constant disappointment and despair. Those who accepted the cruelty of reality as it was and expected nothing from it preserved strength, dignity, and resistance. By detaching from false hopes, they endured where others were broken.

Expectation is the most dangerous chain. Freedom begins when it is cut.

Relationships

Expectation poisons human connection. Lovers who expect constant affirmation suffocate each other. Friends who expect reciprocity fracture when it is not returned. Parents who expect children to fulfill their dreams often drive them away.

History echoes the same truth. King Lear, in Shakespeare's tale, divided his kingdom among his daughters on the expectation of their gratitude. Instead, betrayal consumed him, his family, and his throne. His downfall stemmed not only from their cruelty but also from his blind assumption that love would match his hopes.

These unspoken contract demands, never agreed to, corrode trust and loyalty. Expectation turns intimacy into debt. Relationships collapse not from reality itself, but from the weight of what one side insisted "should" happen.

Wealth and Power

The same law governs money and power. Entrepreneurs who expect loyalty from customers or partners collapse. Investors who expect markets to rise without end are crushed in downturns. Builders who expect effort alone to guarantee reward burn out in silence.

History leaves corporate tombstones as warnings. Blockbuster expected customers to keep coming through their doors, ignoring the shift toward streaming. Kodak expected film to remain forever, blind to the digital future. Both assumed permanence, and both collapsed when the world moved on without them.

Wealth is built by preparing for failure, not assuming success. The strongest systems assume nothing is permanent, including themselves. The builder who detaches from expectation can pivot, adapt, and survive storms. The one who clings to guarantees is destroyed by them.

Human Nature

People act out of their own needs, fears, and incentives, not yours. Expectation is projection: forcing your script onto their reality. Mastery begins when you strip away that illusion and see people as they are, not as you need them to be.

Observation replaces assumption. Calculation replaces disappointment. Detachment replaces betrayal before it happens.

Practical Application

- Strip away every "should" before entering a deal, relationship, or conversation.
- Begin each day assuming no one owes you anything, not respect, not loyalty, not understanding.
- Treat loyalty as a bonus, not a guarantee.

- Build systems with redundancies so betrayal or collapse cannot destroy you.
- Judge outcomes by how you respond, not by what others deliver.

Law-Like Close

The one who expects nothing cannot be broken. Power begins where entitlement ends.

"He who angers you conquers you."
Elizabeth Kenny

LAW 2: Quiet Restraint

The loudest person loses. Control of emotion is control of power in every arena.

History

In 490 BCE, the Persians invaded Greece. At Marathon, the Athenians faced a larger force. Some generals argued to strike immediately; others, blinded by fear and rage, demanded retreat. The commander Miltiades waited, observing the enemy until their cavalry moved to sea. Only then did he order the attack. His restraint allowed the Athenians to fight on favorable ground and win.

History is filled with the opposite lesson, too. Alexander's successors, fueled by anger and pride, rushed into battles they could not win and shattered his empire. Emperors, undone by jealous rages, killed their most loyal allies, leaving themselves exposed. Rage, envy, and pride have ended more reigns than swords ever have.

For enslaved people, restraint was often the difference between life and death. Anger could invite brutal punishment. Open defiance could mean execution. Survival demanded learning to hide emotion, to swallow rage, mask despair, and wait for moments when action could matter.

Even in that brutal system, emotional restraint became a form of power. Songs carried hidden resistance. Smiles concealed strategy. Patience preserved strength until escape, rebellion, or survival was possible. Restraint, under oppression, was not weakness; it was a shield.

Across empires and centuries, the pattern repeats: power endures where emotion is contained and collapses the moment it is not.

Relationships

Emotion is the leash that others use to pull you. A jealous lover becomes predictable. A friend who cannot restrain anger becomes exploitable. A rival who knows what offends you controls you with a word.

Cleopatra understood this. She provoked emotion in others while guarding her own. Rome's most powerful men bent to her influence because she revealed little and read much. In personal ties, the one who reacts emotionally first is the one who cedes power. Calmness is not indifference; it is strategy. The first person to lose composure loses leverage.

Wealth and Power

Markets punish emotion. Investors who panic in downturns sell at the bottom. Entrepreneurs who pursue deals driven by greed often sign contracts that bind them for years. Leaders who lash out in anger destroy teams and cultures that took decades to build.

Napoleon, brilliant in strategy, met his end partly because he could not restrain his pride. His impatience drove him into Russia's winter, a decision that cost him his empire. Wealth, like empires, collapses when decisions are driven by fury or fear.

Sport delivered the same lesson. In the 2006 World Cup Final, French captain Zinedine Zidane, one of the greatest to ever play, allowed an insult to pierce his composure. With millions watching his final match, he headbutted Italy's Marco Materazzi. He was ejected, his team lost on penalties, and his legendary career ended in disgrace. A lifetime of discipline erased in seconds of rage.

Former Uber CEO Travis Kalanick offers another warning. His unchecked aggression and emotional outbursts poisoned company culture and forced his resignation. His empire survived, but his power was stripped because he could not master his impulses.

Human Nature

People expect a reaction. They provoke to test control and reward restraint with fear. The master of power absorbs insult, betrayal, or praise without rushing to show his hand.

Restraint does not mean silence forever; it means choosing the timing and tone of response. To restrain emotion is not to feel less, but to reveal less.

Practical Application

- Pause before responding to provocation; delay is leverage.
- Train yourself to breathe, wait, and decide, not react.
- In conflict, let the other side reveal their emotions first.

- Use others' emotions as information about their weaknesses.
- Never argue in anger; what you say cannot be unsaid.

Law-Like Close

Emotion is the leash.
Whoever controls it controls the outcome.

"The man who cannot command himself will always be a slave."
Goethe

LAW 3: The Leash of Desire

Control appetite or be controlled. Lust makes you predictable.

History

Desire has undone more leaders than armies. Samson, blessed with unmatched strength, fell to Delilah not in battle but in bed. After days of pressing him, she coaxed from him the secret: his hair was the source of his power. One night as he slept in her lap, she called for a servant to cut it. When he awoke, his strength was gone, and the Philistines bound him in chains. Samson was not defeated by force. He was conquered by desire.

Mark Antony, bound by passion to Cleopatra, abandoned strategy for lust and fell to Octavian's rise. Kings across centuries sacrificed kingdoms for concubines, leaving their nations vulnerable while they pursued pleasure.

Slavery revealed another side of desire: power wielded through exploitation. The master's lust was a weapon, a reminder that those who cannot command themselves are driven by appetite, not discipline. The enslaved were forced to navigate that brutality, turning silence, avoidance, and hidden resistance into survival strategies.

History repeats: where lust rules, power dissolves.

Relationships

Lust blinds judgment. A man who cannot restrain himself becomes easy to manipulate. Lovers who exploit weakness in desire hold control over those entranced by it. Affairs have toppled families, destroyed alliances, and left even the strongest humiliated.

Self-control is not repression; it is clarity. To see beauty without losing reason, to feel desire without surrendering choice, is the mark of strength.

Wealth and Power

Power has collapsed in the same way. Bill Clinton's presidency was scarred by scandal. CEOs and politicians have been forced to resign over affairs or harassment claims.

Tiger Woods stood as the most dominant golfer in history, a billion-dollar brand built on discipline and perfection. Then came revelations of affairs and addiction. In days, sponsors cut ties, his reputation collapsed, and his dominance on the course crumbled. A lifetime of mastery was undone not by rivals, but by unchecked desire.

The age of platforms has gone further; it has industrialized lust. Social media feeds are engineered to trigger it: Instagram Explore pages filled with bodies, TikTok's algorithms rewarding thirst traps, Twitter/X running like a hidden porn empire. These platforms prey on attention by weaponizing desire. The more consumed you are, the less capacity you have to create, focus, and build.

Entire industries now run on lust. OnlyFans has become one of the fastest-growing companies in the creator economy, monetizing loneliness and turning weakness into corporate profit. Porn platforms capture billions of hours of human focus every year, trading discipline for dopamine.

For men especially, unchecked desire is no longer just a private vice; it is a marketplace that bleeds their energy, their money, and their will to grow. Every scroll into temptation is stolen time from mastery. The man consumed by lust cannot build consistently; his will is fractured.

The lesson is brutal: the one who cannot restrain desire will be conquered by it, not only by individuals, but by entire systems designed to exploit it.

Human Nature

Desire is predictable. Temptation is the oldest trap. Those who seek to exploit others rarely need armies, only seduction, flattery, or a promise of pleasure.

To master desire is to cut one of the strongest chains of control. To fail is to give others the key to your downfall.

Practical Application

- Discipline appetite as strictly as ambition.
- Treat restraint as strength, not denial.
- Remember that lust is leverage in the hands of others.

- Avoid environments designed to exploit desire (porn, endless temptation feeds).
- Channel desire into purpose, creation, building, and focus.

Law-Like Close

He who cannot master desire will always be mastered by others.

"Time discovers truth."
Seneca

LAW 4: Time is Leverage

Noise demands urgency. Power comes from waiting.

History

Rome did not conquer in haste. Its armies moved slowly, building roads, fortresses, and supply lines. Where enemies sought quick victory, Rome expanded with patience, decade by decade, province by province, until the empire stretched across continents.

Sun Tzu wrote that the wise general wins before the battle begins. To strike too early is to reveal weakness; to wait for the right moment is to strike with certainty. History shows again and again that empires fell not from weakness, but from impatience. Napoleon's rush into Russia's winter destroyed him. Hitler's impatience in opening two fronts cost him his armies. The discipline of time decides more battles than weapons ever will.

Relationships

Patience reveals character. Those who rush into love confuse desire with loyalty. Those who force trust discover betrayal faster. Time is the great filter. It shows who is genuine and who is pretending.

In friendships, in alliances, even in marriage, patience is the only way to see beneath the mask. Those who cannot wait cling to illusions. Those who can wait learn the truth.

Wealth and Power

Markets punish impatience. The investor who panics sells at the bottom. The entrepreneur who forces growth too fast collapses under the weight of debt and overreach.

The collapse of FTX proved the cost of rushing. Sam Bankman-Fried built a crypto empire overnight, fueled by arrogance and urgency. In his impatience to dominate the market, he cut corners, ignored discipline, and gambled with billions. When the truth surfaced, FTX imploded in days, erasing fortunes and exposing the illusion of speed without structure.

Netflix, on the other hand, played the long game. While Blockbuster chased quarterly profits and late fees, Netflix invested in streaming years before the world was ready for it. Blockbuster rushed, tried to pivot too late, and collapsed. Netflix's patience transformed it from a mail-order DVD service into an industry giant.

The modern world screams for urgency: post faster, build faster, sell faster. But the wealth that lasts is quiet, steady, and patient.

Human Nature

Everyone wants fast results. The world rewards the appearance of urgency: hustle, grind, constant movement. But speed without timing is chaos.

Patience is the rarest power because it feels invisible. No applause comes to the man who waits. But the one who can sit in silence while others rush will always have the advantage when the moment arrives.

Practical Application

- Treat time as a weapon, not an enemy.

- Delay response until emotions cool; let others reveal themselves first.
- Play for years, not days, structure systems that survive cycles.
- Resist the pressure of speed from social media, trends, or peers.
- Understand that patience is not waiting idly. It is preparation in silence.

Law-Like Close

Impatience makes you prey. Patience makes you untouchable.

"Power concedes nothing without a demand."
Frederick Douglass

LAW 5: Discernment

Choose your battles. Power is preserved through selection.

History

Power is not measured by how often one engages, but by how rarely one must.

George Washington understood this before the nation existed. Outmatched and undersupplied, he refused the kind of glorious battles that would have destroyed his army. He withdrew, repositioned, and waited. Critics called him weak. History called him victorious. His power came not from confrontation, but from discernment. He chose when not to fight.

Centuries earlier, Rome faced a similar test. Hannibal crushed Roman forces in direct battle. While generals demanded retaliation, Fabius Maximus refused engagement. He delayed, withdrew, and allowed time, terrain, and attrition to erode the enemy. He was mocked for caution, yet his strategy saved Rome. Discernment protected what aggression would have destroyed.

Sun Tzu codified the principle simply. Victory belongs to the one who knows when to fight and when not to fight. The battlefield is chosen long before weapons are drawn. Power begins with selection.

Relationships

Discernment governs human interaction as much as war.

Not every conflict deserves a response. Not every challenge is a test of strength. Those who engage in every argument reveal insecurity, not confidence. Time exposes truth, but only if one resists the urge to rush toward resolution.

Marcus Aurelius ruled the most powerful empire of his era by refusing emotional entanglement. He observed more than he reacted. He chose silence over spectacle. His restraint was not passivity. It was filtration. By deciding what not to engage with, he preserved clarity and authority.

Relationships collapse when discernment is absent. Overexposure breeds familiarity. Familiarity invites disrespect. The disciplined individual withdraws early, not late.

Wealth and Power

Discernment separates builders from gamblers.

Apple became dominant not by releasing everything it could, but by refusing most possibilities. Fewer products. Fewer launches. Fewer decisions. Power grew through subtraction. What Apple chose not to build mattered as much as what it released.

Warren Buffett operates the same way. He allows opportunities to pass without regret. He avoids industries he does not understand. He waits years for alignment. His discipline is not activity, but refusal. Discernment protects capital.

The opposite failure is visible everywhere. Quibi entered the wrong arena. It chased trends, ignored behavior, and burned resources attempting to force relevance. No amount of funding can save a venture launched into the wrong battlefield. Selection determines outcome before effort begins.

Human Nature

People confuse motion with progress. The world rewards the appearance of engagement, not its effectiveness. Platforms profit from reaction. Arguments multiply without resolution. Attention is drained without leverage.

Discernment is the ability to watch without participating. To observe without committing. To withdraw without explanation.

Those who respond to everything are controlled by everything. Power belongs to the one who decides where energy is spent.

Practical Application

- Choose battles before choosing action.
- Refuse opportunities that require urgency without clarity.
- Delay engagement until incentives and intentions are visible.
- Protect attention as carefully as money.
- Withdraw early rather than explain late.

Law Like Close

Not every fight is worth winning.
The disciplined choose the battlefield.

"I have not failed. I've just found 10,000 ways that won't work."
— Thomas Edison

LAW 6: Falling Forward

The strongest builders are not the ones who never fall, but the ones who turn falls into fuel.

History

History does not remember those who never fell. It remembers those who rebuilt with force.

Edison failed thousands of times before creating a working lightbulb. Mandela endured decades in prison before becoming president. Rome burned, rebuilt, and expanded stronger.

For enslaved people, loss was daily life, family, freedom, dignity stripped away. Yet survival itself was resistance, and every act of endurance was a step forward for future generations. Their story proves the greatest leverage often comes from surviving what should have broken you.

Relationships

Loss exposes who stands with you. A failed venture, a public setback, a personal mistake, these reveal loyalty more than success ever could.

The detached and disciplined see loss not as final, but as filter. True allies remain. False ones reveal themselves.

Wealth and Power

In business, collapse is often the beginning of reinvention.

- **Apple** nearly died in the 1990s before Jobs' return rebuilt it into the world's most valuable company.
- **Netflix** shifted from DVDs to streaming after years of struggle.
- **Airbnb** and **Uber** were mocked, rejected, and sued, yet each setback taught them to refine their models until adoption became inevitable.

Kanye West, now known as **Ye**, offers a modern reminder. At his peak, he lost brand partnerships worth billions, was ridiculed publicly, and dismissed as finished. But instead of disappearing, he rebuilt through creativity and independence, leveraging loss to create more control over his art and empire. His collapse stripped access but restored control. Loss removed permission and forced independence.

Even Wall Street operates on this law: bankruptcies clear the weak and allow stronger builders to rise. Loss is not failure. Loss is leverage.

Human Nature

People fear loss more than they crave gain. But this fear blinds them to the truth: everyone falls. What separates builders from the broken is whether the fall is final or forward.

Human nature wants to avoid pain. Power grows by using it.

Practical Application

- Redefine loss as tuition, not tragedy. Every fall pays for future wisdom.
- Study failure until it reveals patterns.

- Filter relationships through loss, see who remains when noise disappears.
- Rebuild with adjustments, not bitterness.
- Remember: falling forward means treating every hit as leverage for the next move.

Law-Like Close

The fall is not the end. It is the floor you push from.

Part II – The New Game

"The old road no longer leads to the city."
African Proverb

LAW 7: Money Shift

If you build for stability, you will break. If you build for volatility, you can adapt.

History

For centuries, wealth was tied to land. Kings and nobles passed fortunes through estates. In America, the postwar generation built wealth through real estate, pensions, and stable careers. Buy a house, work 30 years, retire with security.

History shows that stability is temporary. The 1970s oil crisis shattered markets. The 2008 mortgage collapse erased homes and savings. Fortunes built on "safe" bets vanished overnight.

Every era rewrites the rules of money, and those who cling to the old ones are left behind.

Relationships

Money is not just numbers; it is trust. Old wealth was built on long-term institutions: banks, pensions, governments. Today, trust shifts faster. One headline can erase a company's value. One scandal can crash a currency.

Discernment in relationships now applies to money: who you partner with, who you invest through, who you build beside. A single bad tie can cost years of progress. In volatile systems, who you trust matters more than what you know.

Wealth and Power

The old path is work hard, save, buy a house, built wealth slowly. But housing markets are no longer affordable for most. Careers are no longer stable.

The stock market once rewarded patience through buy and hold. Families passed down shares in companies that lasted for generations. Today, volatility has eroded that certainty. Whole sectors rise and fall within a decade. A portfolio built on "hold forever" can collapse when industries are disrupted by technology or regulation.

The new paths are volatile by design: AI creating industries overnight, crypto producing fortunes and collapses, side hustles scaling faster than institutions.

Consider Airbnb. Hotels once believed their dominance was permanent. They owned the real estate, the supply chains, the loyalty programs. But Airbnb built no hotels, it built a platform. While the hotel industry clung to tradition, Airbnb rewrote the rules, shifting billions in value by turning private homes into a global hospitality empire. Patience did not save the incumbents; adaptability did.

Or look at smartphones. BlackBerry and Nokia once owned the market. They believed their models would last, clinging to keyboards and legacy systems. But Apple and Android adapted to the future, turning phones into computers. BlackBerry and Nokia, too slow to change, collapsed from dominance to irrelevance.

And then there is OpenAI. While older tech giants moved cautiously, protecting legacy revenue streams, OpenAI released ChatGPT and ignited the fastest adoption curve in history. Companies too slow to adapt lost market share overnight. In the new game, those who protect the past too long lose the future.

The contrast is clear: the old world rewarded loyalty and time; the new world rewards flexibility and speed.

Human Nature

People crave the security of the old model, but longing for stability blinds them to opportunity. The young who wait for pensions that will never come, or housing prices that will never drop, are playing by rules that no longer exist.

To build wealth now is to accept volatility. Volatility is not a threat. It is the environment.

Practical Application

- Accept that volatility is permanent and structure your finances for adaptability.
- Diversify income streams. One job, one house, one plan is no longer enough.
- Study how wealth was built before, but do not copy it blindly.

- Use technology and new markets, but protect yourself with discipline.
- Never assume the old paths still work just because they worked once.

Law-Like Close

Old wealth waited for stability. New wealth is built for the storm.

"A good name is more desirable than great riches."
Ecclesiastes

LAW 8: The Brand is You

Clout fades. Reputation compounds.

History

In the past, power was inherited through titles, bloodlines, or land. Kings ruled because of crowns. Priests held sway because of temples. Nobles controlled people through names passed down through generations.

History shows that when institutions weaken, reputation becomes the primary source of power. Marcus Aurelius' writings endured longer than his throne. Frederick Douglass' speeches made him a global figure, though he began life enslaved. Reputation is the bridge that carries influence beyond circumstances.

Relationships

In the new world, people do not follow institutions; they follow people. A company's CEO can have more reach than the company itself. A single individual with credibility can outshine entire organizations.

But credibility is fragile. Followers can be bought; respect cannot. The loudest voices attract attention. Inconsistent brands attract attention. Consistent ones attract opportunity.

Relationships today are not just personal; they are digital. The brand becomes the filter through which opportunities, partnerships, and networks form.

Wealth and Power

The old model said: work quietly, let the résumé speak, and institutions would reward loyalty. The new model says: a digital presence *is* the résumé.

Athletes offer the clearest example. Michael Jordan's brand is worth more than his NBA contracts ever were. LeBron James built SpringHill, a media company that will last longer than his playing days. Elon Musk's personal brand moves markets faster than Tesla's earnings reports.

But the reverse is also true. Vine once created overnight stars, millions of followers, massive visibility, and constant attention. When the platform shut down, most of those creators vanished. They had clout but no brand, attention but no leverage. The few who survived, Logan Paul and King Bach, did so because they built personal brands that transcended a single app. The rest disappeared with the platform.

This is the cost of building attention without ownership. When the platform dies, so does the power. Clout is temporary. Reputation is what endures.

Attention is currency. Reputation is leverage. In the new game, the individual is the institution.

Human Nature

People trust faces before logos. They trust stories before statistics. They believe the individual who stands consistent, even if they distrust the corporation behind him.

Human nature has not changed, only the medium. In a world where everyone can broadcast, the power belongs to those who do so with clarity and consistency.

Practical Application

- Define your brand before others define it for you.
- Share a story with discipline, not desperation.
- Use digital platforms to build leverage, not just noise.
- Align a brand with values that can be sustained for decades.
- Protect reputation like capital; it compounds when guarded.

Law-Like Close

Companies fade. Institutions fall. The brand outlives both.

"Never appear too perfect. Never trust anyone completely."
Machiavelli

LAW 9: Quiet Leverage

The strongest moves are invisible until they are irreversible.

History

True power has often worked in silence. The Medici family in Renaissance Florence rarely led armies themselves; they financed them. While kings and generals sought glory, the Medici controlled money, politics, and even the papacy through quiet networks of influence.

In China, court eunuchs wielded enormous power in the imperial palace, not by shouting commands but by whispering in the emperor's ear. Their leverage was invisible but decisive.

History shows that those who win loudly often fall quickly. Those who win quietly endure.

Relationships

Leverage in relationships is not found in control, but in positioning. The one who speaks least often holds the most sway. The friend who listens more than he talks becomes the one everyone confides in.

Quiet leverage in relationships is the ability to withhold, to observe, to influence through timing instead of volume. Attention is a tactic. The one who reacts last often controls the outcome.

Wealth and Power

In business, loud expansion often signals fragility. WeWork boasted of domination, plastering its name across skylines, only to collapse under the weight of debt and delusion.

The quiet players build differently. Berkshire Hathaway rarely brags, yet Warren Buffett's influence moves markets silently. Amazon grew for years before anyone outside tech circles grasped its scale. The leverage was quiet, reinvestment, long-term planning, hidden logistics, until it was too late for competitors to catch up.

Quiet networks reveal the same truth. When PayPal was sold to eBay in 2002, the founders dispersed into silence. There were no flashy announcements, no endless bragging. Yet that network quietly seeded Tesla, SpaceX, LinkedIn, YouTube, and Palantir. The so-called "PayPal Mafia" did not need noise. The leverage was quiet: reinvestment, long-term planning, hidden logistics.

Quiet leverage also explains the power of connectors. The individual who rarely posts publicly may be the one making introductions that alter careers. Influence does not always look like a stage. Often, it looks like a phone call that changes everything.

Human Nature

People expect power to announce itself. They trust what they can see and underestimate what they cannot. This is the opportunity.

Quiet leverage works because human nature craves spectacle. While the crowd watches noise, true power works in shadows. The builder who plays the long game behind the curtain often emerges with more than the one performing under lights.

Practical Application

- Build networks before you need them. Leverage grows in silence.
- Avoid the temptation to announce moves too early; let results speak.
- Invest energy into systems that compound quietly.
- Use silence strategically; absence can be more powerful than presence.
- Remember: the strongest leverage is invisible until it cannot be ignored.

Law-Like Close

Noise entertains. Silence decides.

"Be careful not to become what you fight."
Friedrich Nietzsche

LAW 10: Reinvent or Die

Clinging to the old self is death. Reinvention is survival.

History

Rome itself reinvented. What began as a republic became an empire, reshaping its institutions to match its ambitions. Power does not punish failure. It punishes stagnation.

In the East, samurai culture transformed after the end of feudal Japan. When the sword lost dominance, many reinvented themselves as bureaucrats, traders, and leaders in a new order. Reinvention preserved legacy when tradition alone could not.

For enslaved people, reinvention was forced but also powerful. Stripped of language, land, and freedom, they remade identity through new culture — blending African traditions with new realities to create music, food, faith, and family structures that endure to this day. Reinvention turned survival into cultural power.

Relationships

Reinvention governs people as much as empires. The partner or friend who refuses to grow clings to a version of themselves that no longer exists. Relationships fail not always from betrayal, but from refusal to evolve.

True loyalty is not to who someone was, but to who they are becoming. The ability to reinvent, shed ego, update habits, and evolve roles determines which bonds survive.

Wealth and Power

The greatest companies are not those that stayed the same but those that shifted identities when the world demanded it.

- **Netflix** began with DVDs by mail, then reinvented itself for streaming, then for original content. Each reinvention killed the old Netflix to give birth to the new.

- **Apple** was once a failing computer company. Reinvention into music (iPod), phones (iPhone), and services rebuilt it into a global empire.

- **Microsoft** shifted from boxed software to cloud services, reinventing its place in the digital economy.

Individuals prove the same law. **Malcolm X** transformed more than once: from street hustler to prisoner, then into a minister, and finally into a global voice for human rights. Each reinvention demanded the death of an old identity so a new one could lead. His life shows that reinvention is not betrayal of the past; it is the only way to expand beyond it.

The opposite lesson is just as clear. Blockbuster clung to its late-fee model and died. Kodak invented digital photography but refused to abandon film, and lost its empire. Failure to reinvent is refusal to survive.

Human Nature

Humans cling to identity because it feels safe. But identity can become a trap.

You are not fixed. You are either evolving or expiring. Reinvention requires humility, the willingness to admit yesterday's self cannot win tomorrow's game.

The paradox: those most afraid of losing themselves end up losing everything. Those willing to shed skin, evolve, and rebuild survive eras.

Practical Application

- Audit yourself: what version of you no longer serves the future?
- Kill obsolete strategies before they kill you.
- Reinvent roles in relationships; don't expect yesterday's dynamics to last forever.
- Stay alert to shifts in technology, culture, and economics — then evolve into them early.
- Remember: reinvention is not betrayal of the past. It is the protection of the future.

Law-Like Close

Do not cling. Become.

Part III – Playing with People

"Care about what other people think, and you will always be their prisoner."
Lao Tzu

LAW 11: Detachment

Power belongs to the one who does not need the outcome.

History

In ancient courts, the most powerful advisors were rarely the loudest advocates. They mastered the art of detachment, offering counsel without attachment to whether kings accepted it. Desperation signals weakness. Detachment signals strength.

The Stoics built entire philosophies on detachment. Epictetus, born enslaved, taught that true freedom was not control of external events, but mastery of one's own reactions. Detachment became a shield that no ruler could strip away.

For enslaved people, detachment was often the only protection left. Rage could mean punishment. Open defiance could invite death. Survival demanded a kind of emotional control that concealed fury and despair. Songs hid resistance. Smiles masked strategy. By appearing detached, enslaved people preserved dignity and waited for the rare moments when action mattered. Detachment, under oppression, became its own form of power.

Relationships

Detachment in relationships is often mistaken for indifference. In reality, it is discipline.

The desperate friend, the clingy partner, the over-eager ally, all surrender power by needing too much. The detached individual, willing to walk away, holds the leverage. Detachment commands respect because it cannot be manipulated.

Wealth and Power

In business, desperation bleeds out in deals. The one who "must" close a deal loses leverage. The one who can walk away often secures the better terms.

Negotiators know this well. Nations and corporations alike respect those who project calm detachment. Warren Buffett waits years for the right investment, walking away from thousands. Elon Musk uses detachment as strategy, threatening to walk from acquisitions, sometimes even meaning it.

Detachment creates control. The less you need, the more options you have.

Human Nature

Humans are wired for attachment, which makes detachment rare and therefore powerful. This wiring makes detachment rare and, therefore, powerful.

When others rage, the detached observer stays calm. When others beg, the detached partner chooses. When others cling, the detached leader decides. Detachment is not coldness. It is clarity.

Practical Application

- Train yourself to walk away from deals, relationships, and arguments.
- Detach from immediate outcomes; focus on long-term positioning.
- Build self-sufficiency so no single person or event controls you.
- Observe emotions before reacting; detachment begins in the pause.
- Use silence as a tool, absence communicates control.

Law-Like Close

Attachment traps. Detachment frees.

"Character is destiny."
Heraclitus

LAW 12: Stone Over Smoke (Respect Over Attention)

Attention fades. Respect compounds.

History

History is littered with rulers who craved attention but lost respect. Nero filled Rome with spectacle, burning fortunes on performance, yet was remembered with disdain. By contrast, Marcus Aurelius rarely sought the crowd's applause, but his writings and character earned respect that outlived his reign.

Even military leaders knew the difference. Alexander the Great won attention through conquest, but it was respect for his vision and discipline that allowed his empire to hold together beyond charisma alone. When attention replaced discipline, collapse followed. When respect was earned, legacy endured.

For enslaved people, attention was forced upon them through auction blocks, punishments, and public displays of dominance. Their humanity was denied in order to entertain or intimidate. But even in that system, respect was preserved in ways that outlived bondage. Songs, stories, and traditions carried dignity forward. Leaders like Frederick Douglass emerged from slavery not by chasing attention, but by commanding respect through intellect, discipline, and unshakable conviction. Respect endured where spectacle was meant to erase it.

Relationships

Attention attracts, but it does not anchor. The partner who constantly seeks validation weakens the bond. The friend who performs for the group may entertain, but rarely commands loyalty.

Respect is quieter. It comes from consistency, discipline, and boundaries. The one who does not beg for attention often receives it anyway. The one who earns respect is followed even in silence.

Wealth and Power

Modern culture confuses attention with influence. Social media platforms reward volume, not depth. Attention without respect has a short lifespan.

Consider celebrities who dominated headlines for years, only to vanish once the spectacle faded. Attention kept them visible; lack of respect left them disposable.

Platforms tell the same story. Clubhouse surged during the pandemic, with endless hype and millions chasing invitations. For a moment, it was everywhere — pure attention. But when the noise died, there was no depth, no discipline, no respect for the model. The platform collapsed as quickly as it rose.

Contrast that with leaders who built quietly. Jeff Bezos was mocked for years while Amazon lost money, but respect for his discipline and execution eventually outweighed the noise. Nelson Mandela commanded global respect not because he chased cameras, but because his life embodied principle.

Attention may win clicks. Respect wins contracts, allies, and empires.

Human Nature

People crave attention because it feels immediate. Respect requires time. Human nature gravitates toward applause, but applause does not endure. Respect is slower to build, but impossible to erase once established.

The paradox is simple: those who seek attention rarely find respect. Those who seek respect often receive attention as a byproduct.

Practical Application

- Stop chasing visibility; focus on credibility.
- Measure success by who respects you, not who notices you.
- Build boundaries that demand respect — never trade dignity for attention.
- Understand that attention fades quickly; respect compounds over time.
- Protect your reputation as capital; it is the foundation of respect.

Law-Like Close

Attention is borrowed. Respect is owned.

"Appear weak when you are strong, and strong when you are weak."
Sun Tzu

LAW 13: Silent Wins

The loudest victory is often the weakest. True power leaves no trace.

History

The highest form of power has never needed applause.

Sun Tzu taught that the supreme art of war is to subdue the enemy without fighting. The greatest victories were achieved before blood was spilled through positioning, deception, and restraint. When the battle never happened, resistance had no shape to fight back against.

Rome understood this principle deeply. Many enemies surrendered before legions ever marched. The empire's reputation alone became a weapon. Victory did not require noise because inevitability had already done the work.

For enslaved people, silence was not weakness. It was survival. Songs carried coded instructions for escape. Quilts stitched with hidden symbols pointed the way north. Small acts of sabotage slowed work in the fields. These victories were never announced because announcements invited punishment. Power lived in quiet endurance, in progress hidden from the eye, in hope preserved without spectacle.

History repeats the same lesson. Noise follows hollow victories. Silent wins endure because they are rooted in inevitability, not performance.

Relationships

In relationships, noise often signals insecurity. The braggart hides weakness. The desperate lover announces devotion. The manipulator oversells loyalty.

Quiet confidence needs no advertisement. The one who does not compete for attention, who delivers without fanfare, who lets actions speak, often commands the most respect. Betrayal and loyalty are revealed not by what people say, but by what they do when no one is watching.

Those who win quietly are remembered longer than those who shout.

Wealth and Power

In business and culture, the most dangerous players rarely announce themselves.

While startups scream about disruption, quiet builders move unnoticed. Google appeared as a blank white page while competitors flooded the screen with headlines and noise. That restraint built trust. That trust built dominance. By the time the world noticed, the game was already decided.

The contrast is consistent. Quibi launched with a billion dollars, Hollywood backing, and endless noise. Months later, it collapsed. TikTok grew quietly, fueled by obsession and word of mouth, until it became unavoidable. Noise brought attention. Silence built an empire.

The same rule governs influence. The individual making private introductions, funding quietly, or shaping outcomes behind closed doors often holds more power than the loudest voice on the stage. Influence does not always look like visibility. Often, it looks like a single phone call that changes everything.

Human Nature

People crave spectacle. Applause feels like power. Performance feels like control.

But noise invites scrutiny. Mystery invites projection. The less you reveal, the more others imagine. And imagination builds reputations larger than any announcement ever could.

Power grows when it is underestimated.

Practical Application

- Do not announce plans. Let results reveal them.
- Use absence strategically. Silence creates gravity.
- Control access. What you withhold matters more than what you show.
- Build quietly until movement becomes irreversible.
- Remember that winning without noise is not invisibility. It is restraint.

Law Like Close

Noise is a performance.
Silence is a victory.

"You must understand human nature, for there is no other foundation of politics than this."
— Niccolò Machiavelli

LAW 14: Human Nature

The one who understands people rules them.

History

Rulers who lasted studied human nature, not ideals. Machiavelli wrote *The Prince* not as poetry, but as realism; men are selfish, ambitious, and afraid. The ruler who pretended otherwise fell. The one who understood it, endured.

In Rome, Julius Caesar rose not only through armies but through his ability to read envy, loyalty, and ambition in those around him. His downfall came when he misread the envy of the Senate.

For enslaved people, human nature was studied out of necessity. To survive, they had to read moods, tempers, and dangers of enslavers with precision. A look, a gesture, a silence could signal safety or violence. But it was not only defensive. Human nature was also a tool for resistance. Escape often depended on predicting which guard would sleep, which overseer was careless, or which ally could be trusted in silence. Understanding human nature was not just survival; it was the first step toward freedom.

Relationships

Human nature does not change in relationships. People are driven by ego, envy, fear, and desire. The one who expects perfection will always be disappointed. The one who studies patterns will rarely be surprised.

- The flatterer wants something.
- The jealous friend will betray when pressure comes.
- The insecure partner will test loyalty again and again.

Mastery is not in controlling others but in seeing them clearly. When you understand motives, you can predict behavior. When you can predict behavior, you control outcomes.

Wealth and Power

In business, fortunes are won and lost by those who misread people. Leaders who over-trust flatterers collapse. Founders who ignore envy inside their teams face betrayal. Nations fall when rulers mistake fear for loyalty.

Theranos provides the modern parable. Elizabeth Holmes built a company on attention, secrecy, and illusion, convincing powerful allies with black turtlenecks and bold promises. For a time, she manipulated human nature brilliantly, appealing to greed, ambition, and fear of missing out. But she misread the limits. Human nature is wired for suspicion. Eventually, doubt grew louder than belief, and the empire collapsed under scrutiny. Attention could be tricked. Human nature could not.

The builders who endure design systems around human nature, not against it. Contracts exist because trust is fragile. Checks and balances exist because ambition never sleeps. The wisest leaders assume people are self-interested, and then use that to align incentives.

The Constant

The paradox is simple: people rarely change, only the stage changes. Ancient kings, modern CEOs, influencers on social media, all move by the same forces: pride, insecurity, greed, loyalty, envy, and fear.

Understanding human nature is the ultimate leverage. With it, you can forgive betrayal before it happens, avoid being blindsided by envy, and align ambition so others serve your vision willingly. Without it, you stumble through illusions, shocked each time reality shows itself.

Practical Application

- Assume people are self-interested, then align their interests with yours.
- Stop expecting loyalty; design systems that make betrayal costly.
- Watch insecurity; it disguises itself as anger, gossip, or overconfidence.
- Study envy; it is more dangerous than hatred.
- Remember: people reveal themselves in small patterns; study those, not words alone.

Law-Like Close

Do not fight human nature. Master it.

"What is not built to last will not last."
Unknown

LAW 15: Ten Years Ahead

Power lasts when it no longer depends on your presence.

History

Empires endure only when systems outlive rulers. Rome fell when its machines of taxation, roads, and legions broke down. The Great Wall of China, though never perfect, represented a system of defense across centuries, not a single reign.

For enslaved people, survival systems were often hidden in plain sight. Songs, networks, and family structures carried memory and identity across generations. The individual might fall, but the machine of culture endured.

Relationships

In relationships, a silent machine is trust built over time. A bond that does not require daily reassurance but moves on rhythm and principle. A relationship that needs constant reassurance is already unstable.

Noise needs energy. Machines sustain themselves.

Wealth and Power

The greatest builders are remembered not for their effort, but for the systems they left behind.

- **Henry Ford** built assembly lines, the machine of industrial scale.

- **Amazon** runs on logistics systems so vast they feel invisible, a machine that delivers without Jeff Bezos in the room.

- **Google** and **Apple** run ecosystems that compound value even when founders are gone.

- **McDonald's** became the global symbol of franchising. Ray Kroc didn't just sell burgers, he built a system where processes were so consistent that the same product could be delivered in any city, any country, by people he would never meet. The machine outlived the man.

The opposite lesson is everywhere. WeWork collapsed because it was built on personality, not systems. Countless influencers flame out because their brand depends on daily noise, not a silent machine that multiplies quietly.

Power is fragile when it depends on your presence. It becomes permanent when it works without you.

Human Nature

Humans crave applause because it feels immediate. But applause does not sustain. A machine sustains.

The paradox: people will always cheer the performance, but they will always respect the builder who steps back while the system runs itself.

Practical Application

- Ask yourself: if you disappeared tomorrow, what would still run? That is your silent machine.

- Build structures, not stunts. Systems multiply; effort burns out.
- Build assets that work without daily presence.
- Automate what you can; delegate what you cannot.
- Protect processes more than performances. The crowd forgets the show; the system endures.

Law-Like Close

Noise dies with you. The machine lives without you.

Epilogue: The New Arena

Power has never disappeared. It only changed arenas.

Rome rose on discipline and order, then collapsed under indulgence and excess. Egypt built pyramids that touched the sky, then fell into the sand. Kingdoms carved borders with blood only to see them erased by new empires.

For enslaved people, power was stripped bare. Names lost. Languages broken. Futures stolen. Yet even in chains, they remade identity through song, faith, and vision. They built culture from ashes. They proved that power is not position, it is endurance. The code carried forward when everything else was taken.

The old world moved slow. Centuries passed before an empire cracked. Today, collapse can come in a season. A company worth billions can vanish in a year. A reputation built over decades can dissolve in a post. The cycles of power no longer turn in centuries or decades, they turn in days.

You've seen it already:

- The dot-com boom burned billions overnight.
- 9/11 reshaped borders and rules of security forever.

- 2008 proved “too big to fail” was a lie.
- Social media crowned kings in weeks and buried them in hours.
- A pandemic shut down the world in a month, erasing the illusion of stability.

And the next shifts are already here. Artificial intelligence writes faster than armies move. Crypto builds nations without borders. Networks of strangers can collapse governments. Leaders now rise not with crowns, but with code and connection.

This is the arena you inherit. Faster. Colder. Louder. More fragile than anything before.

These laws are not tricks. They are anchors. Discipline when the world collapses. Restraint when emotion demands reaction. Systems when effort fails. Respect when attention rots. Vision when others panic.

Noise fades. Attention burns out. Trends collapse. But the code endures, if you do.

Do not mistake this for comfort. The world will not slow down for you. It will not wait. The world will punish noise. It will punish weakness.

But it will recognize builders.
It will bow to those who master themselves when others lose control.

It will follow those who understand people when others misread them.
It will depend on those who build machines while others chase applause.

You are not called to chase. You are called to build.
You are not here to belong. You are here to become.
You are not here to shout. You are here to move quietly, precisely, unshaken.

The code is not written in ink. It is written in action.
It will not live on these pages. It will live in you.

The world will keep shifting. The laws will keep proving themselves.
The code is now yours.
Protect the code. Live it in silence. Let the world learn from the results.

Made in United States
Troutdale, OR
10/01/2026

55119346R00059